Freewheeling

Nine Adventurous Tales of
Boys and Their Bikes

by

Edward Horner

Canadian Outdoor Press

2020 10 9 9 8 7 6 5 4 3 2

Title

Freewheeling; *Nine Adventurous Tales of Boys and Their Bikes*

Publisher

Canadian Outdoor Press

ISBN 978-1-7771539-5-3

Cover photo courtesy of PxHere.com

Introduction
Going Beyond

For a child, the bicycle allows entrée into a world beyond the walking experience - a world just slightly beyond childhood and beyond the familiar neighbourhood. These mechanical marvels allow a young lad, or lass, to travel faster than walking or even running, but slower than the bus or streetcar. It's a personal method of transportation, powered by the efforts of the traveller, at a pace best suited to them. One participates in the act of travel where the journey may be as important as the destination, since, for a youngster, there may occasionally be no destination at all and the journey itself becomes everything.

It's also a world just beyond parental control. Kids are able to travel through and away from their neighbourhood, beyond their normal, everyday experience, away from their parents and often out of sight of adults. It's this ability to, "go beyond," that can often lead to adventures, both positive and negative. Going beyond their comfort zone kids can learn new coping skills, experience new situations, gain some element of independence and apply creative thinking and solve some problems on their own.

For almost every kid growing up in Canada, learning how to ride a bike is second only to learning how to skate at the local rink. In a way, it's a right of passage from infancy where we are completely dependent upon those who raise us, to a more independent being, complete with our own desires and ideas, but now we have the ability to hop on a bike and put those ideas into action. Mind you, it's not like one can't get into trouble without a bike, it's just that bikes made it easier to get into trouble further afield.

Presented here are nine adventurous and entertaining tales from my youth, dating back to about 1967 or 68.

Mishap on the Black Creek
Wet Behind the Ears

I had just passed out of grade 7 and my parents bought me a new bicycle; a gold Super Cycle Racer with the 3-speed Strumey-Archer hub, from the Canadian Tire store on Keele Street. Until this time, I'd been riding around on a dark blue CCM with a single speed, coaster brake, chrome fenders and a streamlined headlamp. I must have put hundreds of miles on that old machine. This new Super Cycle was the key to longer journeys away from home - and further beyond the ever watchful eyes of parents and neighbours.

One such journey found Scott and myself riding downstream along the concrete channel of the Black Creek, in Toronto's West End. This channel ultimately flows into the Humber River after cutting right through the Lambton Golf Course.

I'm not sure when, but likely by the mid 1960s, the creek was confined and streamlined, far upstream - beyond Weston Road, through Trethewey Park and the Old Eaton Estate, as far north as Wilson Avenue, to help control erosion and minimize flood damage. It had, after all, played a major role during the devastation wrought by Hurricane Hazel in 1954, so getting it under control to help protect life and property only seemed wise.

Gone were the lazy meanders and wetlands of the wild creek. Gone also were the natural habitat of birds, otters, beaver and fish. I'm sure today, different choices would be made, but this was the 60s and not a lot of thought was given to environmental damage and quick and dirty solutions were sought.

All this work to avoid flooding seemed to be for not, when, in august of 2005, a heavy rainstorm, later to be known as the *Toronto Supercell*, pummelled many parts of Toronto with high winds and heavy rain. In fact, some 103mm of rain fell in North York, doubling the amount that fell during the devastating Hurricane Hazel. This caused the Black Creek to overflow its banks and flood the basements of dozens of business and hundreds, if not thousands, homes throughout the area. The flood was so powerful that it took out a major culvert on Finch Avenue, causing traffic disruptions for months to come as it was completely rebuilt.

Apparently little thought was given to the aesthetics of is vast, concrete structure. It was utilitarian, cheap and necessary. It was man over nature, pure and simple, brutal and repugnant. Today, it's still grotesque, but at the very least vegetation has overgrown the sides, trees have matured along it's banks and now lean over the channel to somewhat soften it's unsightly harshness. Little bits of nature have re-asserted itself in nooks and cracks along the length of the channel, making it seem less intrusive. Someone, or perhaps some municipal agency, has, in a few locations, placed large rocks and a few boulders in the channel to help break up the monotony of the channeled creek and maybe help make it look more natural. The effort, while appreciated, is not without its irony.

Despite my criticisms of this mini L.A. open drainage ditch, this channeling has produced a nice flat area between the creek and the angled walls of the channel, almost like two sidewalks, one on each side of the creek – perfect for stupid kids riding their bikes in places they shouldn't be.

It must be understood that the channel has a few of small waterfalls along the way. The drops are typically about 6 feet maybe more maybe less, and they seem to be for the purpose of gathering flotsam in weirs that might otherwise end up clogging in the narrow spots – I don't really know. These drops are pretty obvious and easily gotten around, except for the one that is just under the bridge at Scarlett Road - right between the 4th and 12th holes of the *Lambton Golf and Country Club.*

It was late morning – probably August – and the bright sun was casting a shadow from the bridge just across the top of the drop off. Having just gone under the bridge, our eyes hadn't yet adjusted to the increased brightness on the other (downstream) side. Both myself and Scott launched over the edge and fell the 6 feet or so right into the weir below!

By luck, there was nothing but water in the weir below. It could just as easily been the repository of shopping carts, tires, old pallets, etc. but it was empty save for the murky water.

We were both shocked as hell! Neither of us got hurt to any serious degree and our bikes suffered only a few scratches and twisted handlebars. We could just as easily have landed a couple feet to the left and crashed headlong into concrete and done serious damage to ourselves and bikes. We could just have been riding faster and totally overshot the weir and crashed on the concrete beyond – or worse on the far edge of the weir. We were also lucky that the waterfalls itself was little more than a trickle – it could have been much stronger and created a "hole" in which we could have been trapped. We just got lucky.

The water was about 5 feet deep but we managed to drag ourselves and our bikes out of the water. We were soaked, of course, and the bikes needed a bit of attention, but for all that, we continued along the channel through the golf course to the Humber River.

We spent about 30 minutes wading along it's banks, picking up rocks and trying to throw them across the river to the other side. Moving around large rocks to make a bit of a dam to see if we could alter the water flow. Why not? We were already soaked. It was a bright, warm day so there seemed no urgent need to get dry.

Eventually we found ourselves about half a kilometre further down the Humber, where we could see the Lambton/Humber train trestle high above us and a little further south. We climbed back up the bank to the golf course.

In those days, the club wasn't as fancy as it is today and there was lots of building and landscaping going on, so there were muddy or gravelly roads all through the property. We walked our bikes eastward along a gravel road at the edge of the club, back to Scarlett Rd. near the entrance to the course. We were surprised to see a long line of traffic backed up in the north bound land.

It was about an hour and a half later, by now, and we were almost dry. We were just about to ride home when suddenly a couple of bright yellow police cars raced northward down the hill, passed all the waiting cars, sirens wailing, towards the bridge. These two patrol cars joined others already parked. There must have been 8 or 9 police cars there and a small swarm of cops.

Being curious kids, we gave up on the idea of going straight home and we rode down the hill to see what was going on, right past the police cars with no problem at all.

When we got to the bridge, four or five officers with poles, fishing around in the creek, near the weir that we had so recently fallen into. Some were on the bridge, while others were walking down near the water. We asked an officer what happened and were told a couple of kids, on bikes, went off the bridge and into the water. The officer then reaches out and feels my shirt sleeve – of course it's still a little wet.

"How'd you get the soaker kid?"

Sensing that no good would come of telling the truth, I lied.

"Just down by the river sir, messing around in the water."

"Uh huh. Just messing around in the river, eh? So you weren't on this bridge?"

"No sir," we both shook our heads.

8

"How'd you get to the river?" he probed.

"Just along the gravel road," and we both half turned in unison and pointed back up the hill.

I'm pretty sure the cop knew we were lying, but how much time do you spend cross-examining a couple of wet, pre-teen knuckleheads, before you realize you have better things to do?

"Ok. Get out of here. Stay away from the river ... and this channel."

We turned and rode southwards, back up the hill, but not too quickly. We didn't want to look like we were trying to escape.

Any adult might reasonably imagine this episode with it's dangerous fall into turbulent water and a brush with the cops would have a sobering effect on a couple of 12 year olds, but you'd be wrong, as the next tale demonstrates.

Hillside Gardens Adventure
Thirty Feet Across, if it Was an Inch

My friends and I hung around the waters of High Park and Swansea *way* more than we ought to have. There's something about water that's just a constant draw to kids. Maybe not every kid, but certainly for me and my gang. There's a mystery of what lays below the boundary layer between air and water. The ever changing surface texture and the inverted reflections of the trees along the shore and the simple fact that is was largely away from the prying eyes of adults, or more specifically, parents.

One particular day, a few of us; Pantsy, Jim, Byrd and myself were riding our bikes along the top of Hillside Gardens, in High Park, above Grenadier Pond. It was a beautiful, sunny morning, in late August as I recall, for the Canadian National Exhibition was in full swing and we had all been there the day before.

As it so happens, you're not *supposed* to be riding your bike along the top of Hillside Gardens, in High Park – all the signs say so. All the gardeners yell it at you as you ride by. Certainly the police officers on foot patrol take great pains to say so. So, it's not like we didn't know we weren't supposed to be riding our bikes at Hillside Gardens. Yet there we were.

The gardens, lawns, pathways and waterways of Hillside Gardens are situated on the eastern side of the valley of Grenadier's Pond and are quite extensive. The gardens are beautiful – breathtakingly so – and well worth a visit at any time of year. It is especially beautiful in the summer and that of course is only one of the parks many attractions. Another attraction is the rock and pond waterfalls that cascade invitingly (too invitingly it turned out) down the hill just above the boat rental house.

As an aside, it so happens that the gardens are only a stone's throw from the High Park Zoo, which is yet another attraction for kids who are looking for some release from the boredom of their neighbourhood. One winter, a few years later, when I was in high school, Jim, Peter Renzoni and I were doing some ski training on the steep hill that bottomed out at the zoo. We had about twelve bamboo slalom poles that we'd carry back and forth between this hill and our high school about a mile distant. None of us drove so we had to heft them back in our arms. One evening, after training, we didn't feel like walking home with the poles, so we hopped the fence and put the poles behind the mountain goat shelter, inside

12

the chain link fence, intending to retrieve them next afternoon. When we returned the next day, all that was left was a bunch of bamboo splinters! The goats had trampled them, chewed them and generally dragged them all over the enclosure. The poles were now useless, but I digress.

At the bottom of the hill, between the gardens and Grenadier Pond is a large ornamental Maple Leaf (grown entirely of some sort of dark and light purple plants) which seems to pop up on any Google search of Hillside Gardens, High Park. It must be thirty feet across if it's an inch. All beautiful and lovingly cared for by the full-time, professional gardeners who attend the entire garden area.

It was a hot morning. Awful, really. Hot and humid. We had just spent a couple of hours riding around the dirt trails of the park and we needed relief, and that's where the rock gardens and ornamental waterfalls (cascading invitingly) come into the story.

We were kids after all, maybe only twelve or thirteen years old and quite frankly, not particularly bright, and what kid wouldn't want to go into the invitingly cool waters of the ornamental waterfalls? None, I say! So, of course, we got off our bikes, peeled off our shoes and socks, and climbed into one of the numerous pools that graced the waterway.

They didn't have fences up then, for the gardens were relatively new. Either they hadn't gotten to it yet or they didn't think anyone would climb into the pools. Really, they might as well have put up a sign that read, "Swim Here."

So, there were are, the four of us, walking around in one of the upper pools, just wading mind you, nothing mischievous, when a gardener yells at us, "Get out of that water, or I'll set the cops on you!" Being obedient kids, we did exactly what he asked. We scurried a few meters down stream, over a little cascade of water, into the next – lower, pool. We were out of, "that water," but that didn't seem to satisfy the cranky old bugger. Now he starts yelling about this pool! Dutifully, we clamber down into the next lower pool. Still not satisfied, was this gardener. He badgered us all the way down the hill, brandishing a rake, to where the water finally disappears under a service road, before draining into Grenadier Pond.

Ok, we're finally out. He seems satisfied. We walk back up the hill to where we left our bikes on the northern side of the stream, while he walks back, up the southern side, rake in hand, to his wheelbarrow.

Now, the thing about Hillside Gardens is, as I've mentioned, that it offers more than one

14

amusement for stupid kids on bikes. The next most popular thing to do is ride along the hilly and winding cement walkways that thread their way along the hillside. I guess the reason they don't want bikes doing that is – well, it's hilly and twisty and maybe a bit dangerous for pedestrians, what with bicycles speeding past them at breakneck speed. What greater way to hurt yourself or someone else?

We're now more near the southern end of the garden, far away from the water features. Another gardener starts yelling about not riding on the paths. We make our way past the red-faced gardener and around a corner and out of earshot. We head back towards the water features.

As we approach the northern end of the gardens, we see an officer on horseback. He blows his police whistle and motions for us to come over to him. He's on the other side of a fence, further up the hill, near the gardener's house. Jimmy Ears yells out, "Hey! The dick is supposed to be under the horse not on top!"

Holy crap! Why'd he yell that?

Sure, Jimmy Ears' old man had a couple of run-ins with the cops, something about, "Being in possession of stolen property." Occasionally his dad would drop by our house with a new table radio, toaster or maybe some power tools that, "fell off the back of the truck." My dad knew how he got them, and of course, that made him complicit, but ours wasn't a judgmental neighbourhood. Like any street, I suppose, there were certain inequities between families, but not too much. We all had TVs but only a couple of the neighbours had a colour TV. We all had back yards, but only a couple of us had a "patio." No one had too much to brag about.

Any way, after yelling at the mounted cop, Jimmy Ears turns off the path and heads straight down the grass hillside towards the pond, in an attempt to evade the stern looking copper and his horse. I guess we were all little panicked about the officer and we all rode off the pathway and onto the slippery, soft lawns.

Now, if you haven't ridden on a steeply pitched, soft and damp lawn, let me tell you about it. "Control" is only a notion – you don't really "steer" your bike, you more "wish" for your bike to turn in the direction and manner you hope. "Braking" is very much like "steering" in that one doesn't so much do it, as hope it. One dare not even touch the handlebar lever to activate the front brake, for fear it would lock up, slip sideways and send you crashing over the handlebars.

16

So here we are, wishing and hoping our bikes down the slippery, soft lawn of Hillside Gardens in High Park – police officer on horseback yelling at us and the large ornamental Maple Leaf (grown entirely of some sort of dark and light purple plants - thirty feet across if it was an inch) looming closer with each passing second.

Jim was the first to go down as he crashed through the low boxwood hedge that surrounded the circular ornamental Maple Leaf. Following close behind were Byrd, Pantsy and myself. Down we all went – over Jimmy Ears. I was I was in the rear and, apparently, the one with the least intelligence of all, for, having watched all this falling and tumbling over the low boxwood hedge that surrounds the circular ornamental Maple Leaf (grown entirely of some sort of dark and light purple plants - thirty feet across if it was an inch) I did nothing but continue my trajectory into the heap of downed cyclists.

We are now a sweating, soaked, bruised heap, rubbing our knees. elbows, shoulders and shins.

As we're trying to untangle our mess of bikes (pulling pedals from one bike out from between the spokes of another bike), up rides an offer on his Harley Davidson motorcycle – the special "police" model with the gear shifter mounted on the left side of the gas tank and big black running boards for big black, shiny leather police boots, themselves attached to a big leather jacketed, sunglass-wearing motorcycle cop.

He turns off the engine, engages the kickstand with his left foot and leans the bike onto its support. He kicks over his right leg, gets off the machine and starts to help us up and untangle our bikes. He was kind enough to look at our minor wounds and ensure we didn't have any broken bones before he slapped us on the back of our heads, with a leather clad hand, for being stupid and riding in a posted area.

About this time, the officer on horseback had made his way down to the melée. His horse steps effortlessly over the boxwood hedge we had just crashed through and towers over us, with officer Dick looking stern indeed.

With the sound of creaking leather, he dismounts, takes off his sunglasses, pulls his hands out of his black riding gloves, places them both in his left hand and slaps them against his thigh a couple of times while looking us over. "It's Kowalchuk. Officer, Stanley Kowalchuk," he says to us.

He turns and has a quiet word with the motor cycle cop, who almost managed to suppress a

18

laugh. They compose themselves and both turn back to us with dour faces and proceed to make a show of pulling little black notebooks out of their tunic pockets. They began taking our names.

Jim gave his real name, but a fake address, which the officers dutifully wrote down. Byrd does the same. Pantsy continues the charade. Now it was my turn. Don't forget, apparently I'm the least intelligent of the lot. I stammer out my name and fake address. Officer Dick pauses and looks up from his writing, "What's your address again?" I repeat the false information. "I don't think so. There is no 558 Quebec Avenue."

"I meant 585." He shakes his head and looks at the motor cycle cop who looks at me. I'm terrified. I panic and give him my real address.

In a few minutes we're on our way home. Frightened, warned but released on our own recognizance. Bruised, scraped, battered and scratched. I get ribbed about providing a stupid address – what were we expecting – I'm a stupid kid.

For the next couple of weeks each of us, in our own private hell, was waiting for the other shoe to fall. We were certain that at any moment a cop would show up at the front door with a reason for our parents to give us a thrashing. My old man would walk down the street and tell Jim's father that *his* idiot son was involved with his *own* idiot son in some mischief that brought the cops to our house. Then Pantsy's dad and Byrd's old man would get pulled into the fracas and we'd all get grounded or worse.

The funny thing is, no cop showed up. Despite being stupid kids doing a series of stupid things in a place we weren't supposed to be, we managed to avoid the consequences.

When we got back to school in September, one of my classmates, Glenn, sits down beside me on the stone steps of Annette Street Public School, during recess.

"I hear my old man pinched you and Ears in High Park."

"I don't know what you're talking about," I reply.

"My old man chased you in High Park. You got into the fountains, or something."

"I still don't know what you're talking about," I lie.

"My dad is in the mounted police."

"Your DAD is in the mounted police? Your DAD is Kowalchuk?"

"Yeah. I heard about you and Jimmy. Dad said you called him a dick."

"Uh. That wasn't me. I think it was Byrd or Jimmy."

"He and mom had a good laugh over it a dinner. He said you guys nearly pissed your pants."

"No we didn't! We were fine."

"That's not how I heard it. Whatever. It was funny."

"Yeah, I'm laughing."

I remember thinking, "That was too close for comfort."

It must have had an impact on me, for here I am, fifty years later and I can still remember the false address I gave and the fact that Jimmy Ears hurled an unearned, sobriquet at a cop on a horse and only because the officer had a sense of humour did we manage to avoid any consequences.

Map from 1894, showing Catfish Pond (now West Pond) immediately west of Ellis Drive. While Grenadier 'Lake' remains, the two ponds west of Catfish have long since been filled in. The 'Projected' notation (right at bottom of map) refers to the proposed construction and suggested route of electric railways. Note that one proposal has a line running up the west side of Grenadier Lake (now Grenadier Pond) while a second line was suggested up Ellis Drive, itself.

22

Catfish Pond

Bloodied, Soaked and Down, But Not Out

You'll remember that my buddies and I liked to hang around what we called "Catfish Pond" just west of Grenadier Pond, in Swansea, back in the late 60s. Mostly, we built rafts out of the junk we found along the shore and floated around, baking our hides off in the blistering sun. I'm still surprised none of us have developed skin cancer – here's hoping. Any way, Catfish Pond, today, isn't much like Catfish Pond of 1967.

In those days the north-end was pretty much just an open, sloping field, down to the water's edge. There was a path or sidewalk (I can't recall exactly what it was) about half way up the hill. We used to ride our bikes at break-neck speed down the hill, from the sidewalk, and careen totally out of control, into the brackish pond water. It wasn't too deep right at that spot, so after we came to a stop, we'd just walk back to the shore, dragging our bikes as best we could.

I'm sure the water was about as contaminated a body of water as anything else you'll find in Toronto, after all, even today, storm water just pours into it from any number of sources. I'd be surprised if it wasn't posted today for being dangerously contaminated.

One hot summer afternoon, when four or five of us arrived, we saw that someone (some kids) had built a bit of a ramp into the water. A ramp consisting of a couple of wooden pallets, plywood, a metal barrel (likely rolled down the hill) and couple of steel wheel rims (also likely rolled down the hill), some water-logged planks and some rusty nails. The ramp went out about, oh, I don't know, maybe 6 feet. The water at the end was now about 5 feet deep – just deep enough to cushion a stupid kid on a bike jumping off a poorly made, junk ramp.

Okay, we're not total idiots. One thing I learned at an early age, was that you just don't go jumping off a dock into unknown water – never know what you're going to land on. After all, my parents had rented a cottage every summer and that was at least one thing that was drilled into my skull. We carefully scoured the water and found no logs, shopping carts, discarded iron fences or anything else to land on. We were good to go.

At first, we just coasted down from a spot short of the sidewalk – offering just enough speed to get off the end of the ramp without the bike getting hung up on the edge. Good fun. We each took a few turns doing this and helping each other find their bikes and drag them out as required.

Kids, being kids, we weren't satisfied with just *coasting* down from short of the sidewalk and soon we were peddling like maniacs down the hill off the ramp and into the water. We were having a great time, really.

As you may have guessed, the ramp finally gave out as Byrd raced down the hill and out over the water. Not sure what, specifically gave way, but suffice it to say that we had to fish a bleeding and disoriented Byrd out of the water after he cartwheeled off the end of the collapsing ramp.

No one knew anything about first aid in those days, so we didn't know *exactly* how to stop the bleeding from his calf. It was a large gash, as I recall, maybe made larger my memory, but it still seemed large.

The best we could do was wrap a shirt around the wound – which by sheer happenstance was the right thing to do. We used Byrd's own shirt since it was black and didn't show the blood as much. Applying pressure directly on the wound actually helped stop the flow of blood.

We retrieved Byrd's bike and helped him back up the hill to the sidewalk and then out onto Ellis Avenue. The closest place we knew to get help was at the life guard station at Sunnyside Beach about half a kilometre down the hill to Lake Ontario.

Still bleeding, but largely able to balance on his bike, we coasted down to the lake shore at the bottom of Ellis Ave. Once there, we got the attention of the lethargic lifeguard at the beach. He had a quick look at the wound and determined it best to take us to the Sunnyside Bathing Pavilion a little east of his station.

He put up his, "Lifeguard Not on Duty," sign and walked us over to the pool complex where he used what I remember being a "skeleton key," and let us in through a door at the west end.

In those days the dressing area was not like it is today. In the area where today there is a restaurant and courtyard, there was the men's dressing area complete with benches and lockers that you could rent for a dime. The dressing areas also had tin roofs running along the aisles for shade as it was open to the sky. On the east side of the main entrance there was the women's area. The two sections emptied out into a fenced area on the south side of the building where bathers of both sexes would walk through to get to the pool, proper.

To make a long story longer, the lifeguard left us with a female nurse on duty who dressed the wound and told us how to take care of it, gave us some extra bandages, etc. We were back out onto the street in about 10 minutes.

Unfortunately when we came back out, Pantsy's bike was missing! We looked everywhere for it, of course, but had to leave the pool complex without it.

Ears had a Raleigh Chopper bike with a "banana" seat and was easily able to accommodate the wounded member of our party, while the now bike-less Pantsy rode the bike of the wounded towards home. It was a long grind to get home, up through High Park and the dreaded steep hill beside John Howard's, Colborne Lodge. It was hot and dirty work

Eventually we came to the public pool in the park and thought we'd at least have a look around for the missing bike – not that we seriously expected to find it. We had almost circumnavigated the pool and tennis courts, when lo and behold, there it was! Resting against the chain link fence at the west end of the tennis courts. Pantsy grabbed it and we peddled away towards home, up High Park Avenue, as fast as we could, which was not too fast as we had to nurse our wounded along as best we could, now that he had his own bike to ride.

Once home we had to explain to Jimmy's mother what had happened. Funny how a collective lie can be concocted so easily - without any collusion whatsoever. Somehow, it just all came out at once. We were being chased by some teenagers and we had to run away through Jackson Lane, behind our houses. Jimmy went behind the bottle factory when the rest of us went behind the furniture factory. Next thing you know, we're picking Jimmy up off the ground, presumably after he crashed his bike. No, we didn't do anything to provoke the teenagers. We don't know why they started chasing us, they just looked scary. We thought maybe they wanted to steal our bikes or something, so we ran away.

Impossibly, Jimmy's mother seemed to believe us. More likely, she just didn't want to know what really happened. She didn't ask why we smelled of stale pond, for example, or why we were so dirty.

You'd think after that adventure we'd give up doing stupid things on bikes, around water, but again, you'd be wrong. You think we'd stop messing around in Catfish Pond, but we didn't. You'd think we'd stop trying to ride our bikes along the narrow stone walls of the duck ponds in High Park. You'd think we'd just get plain tired of falling into murky water. Nope. We were just stupid kids doing stupid things on bikes.

After having one of our bikes stolen, but then recovered, we pooled what little money we had and went down to Canadian Tire to purchase, a locking chain that would secure at least a few bikes together should we need to leave our bikes unattended again. See? We can learn.

Trail, Rails and Fails
One Good Deed

Devil's Dive

In late July, of 1968, Andrew, Scott and myself were riding the dirt trails of High Park. Near the southern of the park, just east of Colborne Lodge, there is a rather steep path that eventually empties out near the SE corner of the park. Very near the end of the path is, what we called, Devil's Dive.

It was called that because the path takes a steep dive downward for about 15 feet. If you were walking, you'd likely want to put out a hand and lean backwards into the hill to avoid taking a tumble. On a bike, that was not an option.

The only practical way down was a headlong rush, over the precipice, just fast enough to avoid getting your pedals caught on the brink, but not so fast as to get airborne. It was a fine line.

All of us had been down Devil's Dive almost countless times before and we knew what we were doing. Still, there is always some element of risk when dealing with sandy hills and narrow trails. This was before the days where bikes had knobby tires and full suspension. We were just riding coaster brake, fixed gear machines and 'handling' in sand was a lot like 'handling' on soft, wet grass, more wishful thinking than practicality.

Scott was first, I followed only a few seconds behind and Andrew, in turn, trailed a little further back still. Scott and I executed the well-practised maneuver and came to a stop. We turned to watch Andrew.

It was clear, almost instantly, that he was going too fast. He came off the top of the trail with just enough speed to get airborne. While in the air, he and his bike, jointly, tipped forward and nose dived into the sand. The bike came to an almost instant stop, while Andrew continued over the bars to land, stomach down, in the relatively soft sand. It was a miracle that he managed to close his eyes, just before impact, but a crying shame that he didn't do the same with his mouth. I suppose that's because he was yelling that last few feet before impact. Anyway, a mouth full of sand and a split lip was really all the damage he sustained.

His bike fared nowhere near as well. After we dragged him up off the ground, we went for his bike. The front forks bore the full brunt of the impact and were bent back far enough that when you turned the handlebars, the front tire could not clear the down tube of the frame. You'd have no problem if your only goal was to ride around in counterclockwise circles, but the idea of riding any distance was completely out of the question.

The three of us walked our bikes up Parkside Drive, across Bloor Sreet, past Keel Street Public School, up through Oakmount Park, (now Lithuania Park), along Humberside Avenue and so home.

We all knew what awaited Andrew; a thorough dressing-down from his father, and the "I told you not to ride your bike on those dangerous trails," from his mom. Both tough enough to bear, but then there was the *coup de grâce*, the final blow ... a bike ban, likely for the rest of the summer. Talk about killing a kid's spirit. They might as well have put one of his legs in a cast. Well, the forks did need replacing after all, so no surprise really, and that meant hoofing it until the bike was fixed - and his father made it abundantly clear, there would be no hurry on that front.

There Was A Time

At one time, Toronto boasted a commuter rail line that rain around the outskirts of the city. Known as the Belt Line, for, like a belt, it encircled the outer reaches of the city from 1892–1894.

It's route took it east from Union Station, then northwards, up the Don Valley, through the Mud Creek Ravine, into and across Mt. Pleasant Cemetery. From there it turned NW, crossed over Yonge St. And sliced through Forest Hill in a westerly direction to the village of Fairbank near what is now Eglinton Ave W. And Caledonia Rd. At that point it swept southwards, (right behind the *Canada Goose* headquarters on bowie Avenue), making its way down towards what is now Liberty Village to finally run east, into Union Station once again. All in all, a distance of about 26km with 10 stops along the way. For a very short time, there was a western loop that service the residents living just east of the Humber River. (See illustration on page 22). The commuter trains ran for a couple of years, but they never managed to make a profit. There were at least a few reasons for this;

First, they charged 5¢ per station traveled to a maximum of 25¢. For 1892 that was *luxe* travel. Then there was the fact that electrified radial streetcars running up and down Yonge St. Provided a more direct route and a much cheaper fare. Finally, and this is probably the most important factor, the land development and population expansion out into the suburbs beyond Eglinton Ave, just wasn't grabbing hold, primarily due to the fact that the country was suffering through a recession in 1893. By the end of 1894, the Belt Line declared bankruptcy and was forced to sell off what assets it had.

During World War I, the tracks on the steep grade through the Moore Park Ravine were torn up, melted down and used in the war effort.

For years afterwards, the land and rails passed from one company to another. Certain sections of track were used for shunting and detouring, but it never again was used for passenger service.

In the 1950s, the TTC used the western section from Union Station to Yonge St. To take

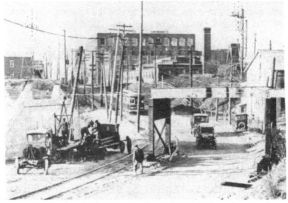

Toronto Suburban Railway is seen here about 1925, realigning their track to accommodate the construction of the Lambton Spur of the Toronto Belt Line railway which crosses Weston Rd, north of St. Clair. Ave. At this time, the TBL was owned by the Canadian National Electric Railway and they ran an electric train from Toronto to Guelph, Ont. (City of Toronto Archives, Series 71, s0071_it4029).

delivery of the new subway cars. They were shunted up from the Lakeshore, through Fairbank, across the section north of Eglinton Ave, through Forest Hill to finally be unloaded in the Davisville yard.

A couple of cars from the CNER makes it's way over Weston Rd, just north of St. Clair Ave. W. The line came all the way in from the Guelph area, almost 50 miles to the west, making it a true inter-city transportation route. It carried passengers, express and freight.

At some point, likely the mid 1920s, there was a Lambton Spur Line that was added, which ran from about where St. Clair Ave. W, and Prescott meet up, at an angle NW to cross Weston Road, north of St. Clair and then roughly parallel to St. Clair (north side), in behind the Swift Premium factory, (now gone) all the way out to the Humber River. It's this little Lambton Spur where our story really begins.

We Meet Walter

Between Symes Rd. and Weston Rd. the Lambton Spur was, by late 1969, largely abandoned. There were still tracks that ran over the Keele Street bridge and the track continued beyond Symes, to the west, as I recall, but I don't think I ever saw a train along this section of track. The ties were rotten, small trees were beginning to grow up between the tracks and the tracks themselves had become very rusted.

If you look it up on a map today, the section of line where this story unfolds is known as *Lavender Creek Trail.* A little further east, across Weston Rd, it's known as *Sandra Park Trail.* In between these two sections there is a storage yard for truck trailers, a municipal maintenance yard and an allotment garden, all nestled under the high tension wires of Ontario Hydro.

Along this section, west of Weston Rd., the track bed traverses the side of a hill. To the south, the land rose quite sharply up to Glen Scarlett Road, which ran more-or-less parallel with the Lambton Spur at this section. To the north, the land fell away quite quickly, down to a wetland area in the bottom of the valley, maybe 30 feet below.

There was then, as there is today, a few light industries located along Glen Scarlet Rd, which of course backed onto the valley, over-looking both the tracks and the wetland.

Between these business and the trackbed there were at least a few narrow footpaths that led downward, across the tracks and then fur-ther down to the wetlands. On the far side of the swampy area there were houses and it could be reasonably assumed that at least some of the workers lived there and these trails were created by their coming and going.

It was a cloudy, cool and wet day in early Sep-tember when Andrew and I found ourselves walking along the rail bed, he in his army sur-plus rain poncho and me in a yellow slicker.

We had taken the Keele trolly bus up from Humberside Ave, where we were hanging out with Tom H. in the morning, and had just got-ten off at Gunn Rd, right where the Lambton Spur bridge crossed Weston Rd. Of course we were taking the bus, as Andrews 'bike ban' was still in effect.

We had been along this particular section of track numerous times before - mostly riding. Sometimes you find things, things that had been abandoned or disposed of by passers-by or from the business up the hill. One of the best finds were round, imperfectly moulded, red plastic reflectors that were too often just dumped over the back fence of a plastic factory rather than being disposed of properly - much to our delight. Our bikes, bike of friends and our bedrooms at home were profusely, if not tastefully, adorned with these reflectors.

We were just going to walk along to Symes Road, turn south and then back out onto St. Clair. With a bit of luck we might get to see the cattle hands drive the cattle from the stock yards on the south side of St. Clair to the slaughterhouse on the north side. When that happens, traffic was stopped, large gates swung open and the cattle driven through. I didn't really understand until a bit later in my life what was really going on in, 'Canada Packers' and 'Swift Premium.'

By this time, you're probably asking yourself, "what has any of this to do with bicycles?" Well, here you go.

Just before we got to Symes, we heard someone crashing through the brush, down a footpath on the hill to our left. In a second or two a boy on a bike, came charging across the tracks on his bike, hitting the rails and cartwheeling off his bike and down the hill on the other side.

Andrew and I looked at each other then promptly ran down the hill to the kid. He landed abut half way down to the swamp. When we got there he was sitting up holding an arm, which was obviously broken, as the elbow didn't seem to bend quite the right way. He was dirty, scratched and cut. Not too surprisingly, he was crying.

We helped him back up the hill, variously pushing and pulling up the loose stone incline, to the trackbed. We didn't understand it at the time, but he was in shock – shaking, lip quivering, not quite sure where he was etc. We didn't know anything about first aid or how to look after an injured person, so we had to get help. The kid couldn't get up and just sat on the track shaking in the rain.

Andrew took off his rain poncho and put it over the kid and said he'd go for help on the kids bike. Now, this would have been a Saturday or Sunday, so the nearest help would have been to ride along to Symes Rd, up the hill, past the incinerator, (closed up tighter than a drum) and out onto St. Clair Ave.

Andrew took off, now wearing my yellow rain slicker. I stayed with the kid, the two of us sheltered under the rain poncho.

I managed to learn his name, Walter - Walter K. He was a year younger than me, thirteen.

The Symes Rd. Destructor (incinerator) disposed of solid waste by burning at high temperatures. Construction began during the Great Depression and was complete by the time this photo was taken in 1934. The Art Deco style adds quite a flair to such a utilitarian building. (City of Toronto Archives, series 372, s0372_ss0070_it0447)

He lived on Mavety Street, south of Humberside. He went to Keele Street Public School, etc.

It seems he was just exploring along the back of the chainlink fence behind the business on Glen Scarlett when he rode down the footpath, lost control in the mud, and crashed.

He seemed to be going in and out of his shock as he had moments of lucidity interspersed with shivering, dizziness and some confusion. It was obvious he was in quite a bit of pain. I just kept telling him it would be OK, my friend had gone for help and will be back soon.

About 15 minutes later, Andrew re-appeared on Walter's bike, followed closely by a yellow police car. The police were able to drive in from Symes a short distance, but had to stop as the space between the tracks and the north side hill got too narrow. They jumped out and quickly walked along to where we were sitting.

They managed to get a little more information from Walter before piling us all into car, bike in the trunk, and taking us to St. Joseph Hospital.

Once there, Walter's parents were called and they arrived in very short order. They were overcome with concern, grief, anger, happiness all at once. "What was he doing there? He knows better. Oh we're so happy you helped him. Don't ever do that again, etc."

While all that was going on, the police took our statements and we called home. The officers talked to our parents told them that they'd give us a ride home when they were finished at the hospital.

"No, no Mrs. Horner Eddy isn't in trouble. No, not at all. No, really. Yes, hard to believe, I'm sure. He's been very helpful."

All in all, a fairly adventurous day.

About a week went by and both Andrew and I had pretty much forgotten about the whole incident. Then one day, Andrew gets a knock on the door. His parents answer and it's the parents of Walter, the kid we helped. Learning that Andrew had previously wrecked his bike, seemingly beyond repair, they bought a used one for him as their way of saying thanks for helping Walter.

Within a few minutes, my father was talking to Walter's parents over the backyard fence in Andrew's backyard. It seems they'd gotten me a Wilson, A200 baseball glove in way of thanks. While I wasn't much of a baseball fan, which was a rare thing in those days, I did enjoy playing a bit of catch with the old man.

My parents and Walter's parents became friends and we'd have them over to the house a couple times a year. Walter ended up going to Western Tech, while I went to Humberside Collegiate, so we had some contact and get togethers with Andrew over the years. They moved away, to the US, just before I went to college. While Walter and I kept in touch for a while, it's been at least 25 years since we've touched base with each other. I truly hope he's doing well.

Going Once, Going Twice
Learning to Fall, All Over Again

In the summer of 1970, Tommy H. and I went to a police auction on Strachan Avenue, near King Street. We hadn't been to a police auction before, so we didn't really know what to expect, we didn't know what they'd have or how much anything might sell for, so we were open to just about anything.

It was held in a large building, maybe a police garage for vehicle maintenance, on Strachan Avenue, just south of the train tracks. In those days, Strachan crossed the tracks on the level. There was about 6 or 7 sets of tracks that you had to negotiate in order to get to the other side. Today, of course the tracks have been "sunk" and Strachan goes over them on a modern, wide concrete bridge. The building in which the auction was held, is, surprisingly, still standing at the SE corner of Ordnance and Strachan, although it's changed quite a bit. It's now broken up into little business, studios and offices.

The auction began about noon and the garage was fairly crowded. Old people, young people. Men dressed in business suits rubbed shoulders with rough labourers. Men and women from all walks of life seemed to be there. Most of them had pencil and paper in hand and were busy scribbling.

There were a few canoes, a bunch of bicycles, some kitchen tables and chairs, a couple of motorcycles and other assorted goods all housed in the building. Each item, or group of items, had a number on them and it seemed you bid on the number corresponding to the item. They didn't bring each item up to the platform, but rather just announced, "Item 544 a canvas canoe. Bidding starts at five dollars," or something along those lines.

I think the vast majority of the people in attendance were there for the cars and pickup trucks parked outside. There was about twenty vehicles parked on the curb and on the space between the road and the building. These vehicles had numbers, just like the other goods. When we arrived, dozens of people were pouring over the vehicles, looking under the hoods, turning over the engine, checking inside and kicking the tires.

The auction began with the vehicles. The bidding was quick and furious. The cars and trucks were sold in a matter of thirty or forty minutes. When that was over, the place pretty much emptied out except for a dozen or so hangers on. All that remained was the furniture, canoes and bicycles.

The bicycles were next. Tommy and I had looked over the bikes when the bidding for the vehicles was underway and we made note of the numbers of a couple of bikes that might be of interest if the price was right. Having worked at odd jobs all summer and saved almost every cent of my weekly stipend, I had fifty bucks in my pocket and Tommy had about the same. We didn't think we'd be able to buy anything as the bikes looked rather pricey, but we'd try.

One bike caught my eye. A Gitane, Tour d'France. It had a little picture of a man's face on a sticker and the name, Jacques Anquetil and a signature beneath it.

"Hey Tommy. Isn't this the kind of bike Anquetil won the Tour d'France on?"

"I don't know. Maybe. Yeah, I think so." He hefted the bike by the seat and handlebars. "Light. Looks in good condition. Good bike. Too small for me." Indeed it was too small for him. Tommy was probably 6' even in high school and would have required a much larger frame.

I looked the bike over in further detail. Reynolds 531 tubing, Simplex derailleurs, Mafac brakes with Mavic clincher rims on Normandy hubs. Michelin tires. The wheels spun fairly true, nothing a bit of spoke tweeting wouldn't fix. The derailleurs both worked smoothly. Simplex drop outs. It was clean, only a few scratches, no obvious mis-alignment in the frame. I straddled the cross bar and the frame just grazed my crotch - perfect size. It had toe clips on the Pierre Lyotard, Berthet pedals which I had seen in pictures of course, but never up close. These odd pedals also had a lip on the back to make it easier to insert your shoes.

"This might be worth bidding on. What'd you think?" I asked.

"Yeah. It looks good."

An amplified voice broke in our our quiet conversation.

"Item 667. A ten speed bicycle. Biding starts at five dollars, in five dollar increments."

I was rather taken by surprise. One of the other bicycles I was interest in was the first one up for auction, a gold Raleigh. Tommy had to elbow me into action when the bidding got to twenty dollars.

"Twenty five!" I yelled.

"I have twenty five. Do I hear thirty?"

"Thirty," came a voice from behind.

"Thirty five," came another voice.

48

"I Have thirty five. Do I hear forty?"

A long pause. What should I do? It's not the first choice of bikes I had my eye on. I really wanted the Gitane. I stayed silent.

"Forty? Anyone with forty?"

Another pause.

"Going for thirty five.   Once ... twice ... SOLD for thirty five."

Other bikes came and went for prices more or less. There was probably about a dozen before item 680 came up for auction.

"Item 680. A ten speed bicycle. Bidding starts at five dollars."

I jumped on five dollars.

Then voices from around me shouted, *"ten," "fifteen," " twenty," "twenty five," "thirty," "FORTY."*

What? How'd it to go high so fast? It took seconds. I panicked.

"FIFTY!" I yelled. There was a bit of agitation in the small crowd. I heard some mumbling.

"I have fifty. Do I hear sixty?"

A pause.

"Do I have fifty five?"

Another pause. I could feel my heart pumping faster and a tightness in my stomach. The pause seemed to go on longer than all the other final pauses. Was the guy doing this on purpose? Was it really longer, or did it just feel like that?

"For fifty dollars. Going once ... going twice ... SOLD for fifty five dollars. Next is item 681 a ten speed bicycle. Bidding starts at five dollars."

Tommy nudges me. *"You got it! You friggin' got it man! Let's go pay the guy and get the bike."*

Merde. I actually did get it. I was almost in shock. In a daze I made my way to the payment wicket. I told the guy the number and he looked down a long list of numbered items. He neatly crossed out the number with pencil and ruler, then gave me a hand written receipt for the fifty dollars and a ticket for item 680. New, in a bike store that machine would have been worth about four hundred dollars. I got it for fifty!

We retrieved the bike, showed the ticket and hand written receipt to the officer at the garage door and left the building. The tires were pumped up, but not hard enough to ride, so Tommy and I walked to a gas station at the corner of Roncensvalles and King. We tried to use their Bennett "Tireflator" to inflate the tires, but for some reason the head of the Tireflator wouldn't fit properly over the valves on the tires. Hmmm …

A closer look revealed that the valves on the tire and the coupler on the Tireflator were completely different. What the heck? We couldn't' really ride the bike and it was a hike home and we had no way to inflate the tires. Fortunately, there was a little bike shop on Bloor, just west of Dundas and we walked up there to get help, maybe about a mile and a half.

The old guy (probably only something like 30) looked at the valve and simply said, *"Presta. You need a presta pump."*

"A what?" Tommy and I asked in unison.

"Presta pump. For the presta valves. You got presta there, not Schrader."

Neither Tommy or I had any idea that there were two types of valves. We'd only ever known the one, and we didn't even know that had a name. *Schrader* - the standard valve in

North America. This was a French bike with crazy valves.

Not only did these French valves look different, but they worked differently from the Schrader. You had to take off the little plastic cap and unscrew the small brass, knurled collar in order to open the valve so that air could be pumped in. When done, you tightened the brass collar and replaced the plastic cap. We had no idea.

Thankfully, the bike shop owner had little brass adaptors that could be screwed over top of the presta valve, after it was opened, and the end would accept a Schrader style pump. I think he charged us a couple of bucks for it. I only remember Tommy had to pay as I had already spent every penny I had in my jean pockets.

We got the tires inflated at the store. Tommy went home on the Junction 40 streetcar and I, after fiddling with the toe clips, rode home with my new Gitane.

The toe clips were of course awkward at first. I didn't really see the point. If the clips were loose enough to slide your foot in, then it was really too loose to offer any performance advantage as the foot continued to slip around. In my mind, they had to be loose enough so that when you came to a stop, you could slide your foot out backwards and put your foot down on the curb so you wouldn't fall over.

I rode the Gitane for a couple of weeks before I bought a copy of Bicycling at McBride Cycle and learned that I was using the toe clips all wrong! They had to be tightened every time you slid in your foot. Once tight, you could apply power through a longer arc of the pedal stroke - even applying a small effort on the upstroke. Another, hmmm … moment.

With that discovery, I did indeed find there was more power over a larger arc of the pedal stroke. I brought my findings to Peter Renzoni, my ski trainer and himself a competitive bike racer. He was a couple of years ahead in school. He informed me that toe clips are great, but they need to be combined with cycling shoes and cleats.

After school, we went to his house and he showed me a very light, thin pair of black leather cycling shoes - Adidas as I recall. They had a rock hard sole that offered no flex at all so that as much energy as possible could be transferred from the cyclist to the bike.

Then came the pièce de résistance, aluminum cleats. These were specially-shaped pieces of aluminum that would slide over the rear edge of the pedal and actually lock the foot into place once the toe clips were tightened.

He explained and demonstrated the art of "ankling" to gain greater power from each stroke of the legs. This is a peddling technique in which one lowers the heel on the down stroke and raises the heel on the up-stroke, smoothing out the muscle contractions and elongating the power stroke of each cycle. It was somewhat like trying to scrape mud off the bottom of your shoe each time your foot reached the bottom of the down-stroke. All terribly technical and I never really got the hang of it. Still, it all made such perfect sense.

One would "wear in" the cycling shoes with a few days of riding with toe clips, sans cleats. A mark would form on the bottom of the shoe where the back of the pedal hit the sole. This mark was then used to align the aluminum cleat where it would be permanently fastened to the sole of the shoe. Once the cleated shoe and toe clips were fastened, one-to-the-other, it made a unified structure which would transfer the maximum amount of power from the cyclist to the machine. Brilliant.

Off I went to Bloor Cycle for a pair of Eddy (Cannonball) Merckx, Adidas cycling shoes and a set of aluminum cleats.

As instructed, I rode the machine with the cycling shoes, without cleats, for a few days to "wear in" the soles. I then took the shoes and cleats to a shoe repair guy on Pacific Avenue that Peter had told me about and had him nail on the cleats using brass tacks. Solid. Bomb-proof.

Home I went, shoes in hand. I kit up and struggle with the intricacies of the entry and exit of the cleated shoe into the toe clips. I'm fairly coordinated and get it down pretty quick. I roll out onto High Park Avenue and immediately feel the power. THIS is what it ought to feel like. THIS was such an improvement in power! It was awesome.

I figure out how to loosen the straps well before a planned stop. I call on Peter and we got out for a quick ride in High Park. We make a couple of laps but Peter had to get back home so we exited the park at the north end, at the Bloor Street gate. The light was red. We pull up to the intersection. Peter casually puts out his right arm and rests against a lamp post, his feet still firmly engaged in his toe clips. I pull up behind him, try to pull out my right foot, but can't. I'm locked in! I forgot to loosen the toe clips as I slowed down. I struggle and wiggle, but my right foot is trapped. Down I go onto my right side, falling onto the side-walk. Peter hears the crash and unclips himself and comes back to help me.

"Yeah. You have to think ahead a bit. Better to just lean against a post if you're stopping at a light."

"Thanks. I think I get it," I replied.

I get untangled and back on my ride. I see Peter home and continue home myself. Before I get to the driveway, I'm careful to loosen the toe clips and twist out my foot.

Despite my precautions over the next couple of weeks, I still had a few tip overs. You learn quickly that if you're going down from a standstill, you lead with the lower half of the body so the large muscles of the thighs and buttocks take the main impact, then you sort of follow through with the upper body.

One memorable tip over was pulling up behind Tommy H. while coming to a stop at a light. He stopped short and nudged in to the curb, not knowing I was right behind him. I jammed on my brakes. I didn't have quite enough room and ran into his rear wheel on the derailleur side, actually hitting his gear cluster. This jams my forks so I cant wiggle for balance and I fall onto a couple of eight or nine year old kids who are standing, innocently, on the sidewalk.

If that wasn't bad enough, I also hit my head on a steel cable that is running up at an angle from the sidewalk to the lamppost (presumably to support the post in some way) and it hurt quite a bit, but bled even more.

It turned out to be only a minor gash on my scalp, but what a bloody mess it made. Blood matted hair, blood dripping down my face, getting in my eyes, off my chin. I helped the kids back to their feet, apologizing as I did so, but they ran away, probably traumatized from the sight of a bloodied, long-haired cyclist.

I had a spare cycling shirt in my shoulder bag and I used that to daub away most of the blood. Tommy then helped wrap my head in the same shirt and we rode to Dr. Varty at the corner of Pacific and Annette for a quick fix of bandages and tape.

The next day I ride over to the Loblaws grocery store for some pasta, a jar of capers, a couple of onions, some parmesan and a tin of tomato sauce. It's one of the large stores with the green terrazzo floors that are always kept polished to a lustrous gloss. I lock up my bike and walk to the store with my cleats. Click, click, click across the cement sidewalk. The automatic door swings open and in I walk. Click, click, click, whoosh! Flat on my back. What the hell just happened?

Apparently walking around on polished terrazzo floors (polished to a lustrous gloss) in hard-soled cycling shoes with aluminum cleats is not a thing people do. They were very slippery and you had to walk with straight legs, on your heels, toes up. Walking like this isn't very stable and when you add the slippery cleats it's an accident looking to happen, and it did.

Any way, I still had a couple of bandages on my head from the incident the previous day and the blood starts to leak through. I forget about the shopping trip and walk up to visit Dr. Varty again, leaving my bike locked at Loblaws. He admonishes me for not taking it easy, re-bandages my scalp, then sends me on my way with a warning that if I come back he'll have to put in stitches.

The next day, I rode back down to Bloor Cycle and bought an Italian-made "hair net" helmet. It was fashioned of a beautifully smooth, shiny, soft black leather, wrapped over some sort of hard foam liner. It was referred to as a "hair net" because it really didn't cover much of the head at all and it had large open spaces, presumably for reduced weight and increased ventilation. There was no real protection in that helmet, but it might have helped in the tip over from a couple of days ago and my slip in the grocery store from the previous day.

This new helmet cost me forty dollars and it looked dorky as hell. Andrew gave me a cotton Bloor Cycling racing cap with a little brim emblazoned with MAVIC. *"Put this on first. You won't look so stupid."* I put on the cap and reposition the helmet. *"Pull it tight here and here,"* he instructed. He stood back to better take it all in. He stepped up and pulled the helmet further forward on my head. He then turned my head left and right. He stepped back again and put his hands in his pockets. He shook his head. *"If you had a John Player hanging out of your mouth, it might look better."*

I always liked Andrew, as he gave such good advice. I kept the cap, but poo poo'd the smoking.

As I recall, that fall over the steel cable was the last time I had any incidents that I could reasonably blame on the toe clips. I finally figured out how to properly use them and equally important, when not to use them.

The Bottecchia Giro d'Italia
Ignorance in Action

W hen I graduated from high school, my parents and I went into Bloor Cycle on Bloor St. W. where we combined our money and bought me a Bottecchia, Giro d'Italia – a quality mid-range racing bike that would, in the years ahead, take me thousands of miles around Ontario – touring, not racing.

Campaign Del Mondo 1966. Columbus steel tubing, hand brazed lugs, partial Campagnolo Record gruppo, optional Universal 68 side-pull brakes, chrome tipped forks and chrome highlighted rear and chain stays, beautiful paint job, etc.

I had the option of equipping my new bike with either clincher tires (the type you are most likely familiar with) or "tubular" tires, also known as, "sew-ups," which offered reduced weight and performance. Price difference was considerable and I opted for the clinchers with aluminum rims, plus I was more familiar with them.

That summer I must have put a thousand miles on that bike. In comparison to my beloved Gitane, this was a thoroughbred of

cycling machines.   Still, as the end of summer approached, I knew I just had to have the
lighter, higher performing tubular tires and
rims.

So I walked over to High Park Cycle where I
purchased a new rim and hub set and had
them lace the wheels for me. I picked the
Campagnolo hubs and Mavic aluminum rims
with double-butted stainless steel spokes – I
had been working all summer and had quite
the wad of cash saved up. High Park Cycle
was even gracious enough to give me a bit of
a trade-in on the old wheel sets. Only reason
I didn't go back to Bloor Cycle was that they
couldn't get the wheels laced as quickly as I
wanted them.

I also purchased three or four tubular tires for
my touring. These had more tread on them
than the "racing" tires they had in stock and
promised to last longer with fewer flats. I
dragged it all home and assembled the tires to
the rims and pumped them up with my high
pressure Silca pump. I immediately recog-
nized that I had to re-adjust the brake pads
and cable length on the Mafac brakes, since
the rims were far narrower than the old
clincher rims.   I successfully struggled
through that little task, threw a spare tire in
my shoulder bag and went out for a ride.

Holy cow! These were a dramatic improvement over the old clinchers. They offered less unsprung weight, they were harder and offered way less rolling resistance – plus they made the bike ride like it was supposed to – tight and fast. My enthusiasm for these tires and rims only increased as the days passed that first week.

Now here's the thing about enthusiasm – it tends to blind us to critical issues. Take tubular tires for example. Despite being all the good things I talked about they also command a little more attention to detail than the old clinchers. Point in fact; tubular tires come with a special adhesive cement that is applied to the cotton backing of the tire and the rim. Once the cement has become almost dry to the touch, they are then rolled onto the rim where they can be inflated and slightly adjusted for a true roll.

It all works perfectly, *if* you follow the instructions. I didn't. For some reason, I thought you only had to apply the glue to the rim, not both the tire and rim. In my enthusiasm, I imagined that you couldn't possibly wait until the glue was dry before pressing the tire onto the rim – how could you reposition it afterwards? I just blithely applied the glue to the rim and rolled the tire over onto it. I let the tires sit overnight so the glue would dry. I thought I was good to go.

Ah, but thinking and being are two very different animals. For that first week, I rode back and forth to work with nary a problem. Then, on the way home on a Friday, I whipped along the road and turned sharply into the driveway of our backyard. The front tire peeled off the rim and the rim hit the asphalt and skidded like I was on ice. I went down like a ton of bricks, crashing into the fence.

I still bear the scars of that crash on my left knee and elbow. The road-rash on the outer side of my left calf and hip has healed nicely and today there is no evidence of that particular injury. The hairs on the back of my neck are standing up as I think back on that crash. Brrrr.

As for the bike; the front rim was crumpled like a pretzel, handle bars were bent, broke the front brake handle and bent the left crank arm. Of course, I couldn't blame myself and tried to pin it on the poor quality of the Hutchinson Super SC tires and Mavic rims.

In the end I knew it was not a failure of my equipment, but a failure of my judgment. It always is.

All in all, it cost about $200 to have it all fixed or replaced. I felt I couldn't show my face at

HPC or Bloor Cycle, so I had it all repaired by D'Ornellas Bike Shop, out in the boonies,

This wasn't so much about being stupid as it was about being ignorant and/or overly enthusiastic. The tires and cement came with complete and detailed instructions for installation and repair. I only briefly scanned them. I could have admitted at High Park Cycle, that I didn't know what I was doing and asked for advice, for if there was one thing the guys at HPC had in abundance it was advice - asked for, unasked for, it didn't matter. They had it in amounts copious and fulsome . If I hadn't been in such a hurry to get my tubulars in the first place, I could have waited an extra few days while Andrew and his crew at Bloor Cycle did the whole job for me. So much for my enthusiasm.

Even now, many years later, when I'm about to start a new project or mechanical task that is new to me, I always think about this little story, as it helps me slow down, evaluate my skills and motivation for the job and reminds me what can do wrong when ignorance and action clash.

Ticket to Ride
Five Dollar Bet

About a month after I got the Bottecchia, I was out riding with Tommy H. We were way out in the west end of Toronto, somewhere near Marie Curtis Park at the bottom of Brown's Line. We were riding back from visiting a friend who lived in a little four story walk-up on one of the numbered streets between Lakeshore Avenue and the Lake.

It was early evening and we had just wheeled up one of those numbered streets and onto Lakeshore Avenue, eastbound for home. I was ahead of Tommy by a few seconds when I turned right onto Lakeshore into the waiting hands of a cop. Not literally, of course, but there he was, just standing by the side of his patrol car, waiting for … something. I guess I was it.

He stepped out into the road, directly in front of me, forcing me to a complete stop.

"What's the problem officer?" I enquire.

"You didn't stop at the stop sign."

"Really? I slowed right down and looked before I came out. I thought I stopped."

About this time, Tommy comes wheeling up from behind me. He had seen the cop and he had managed to come to a complete stop at the corner.

The officer starts writing out a ticket. He asks me for a piece of ID. I give him something like a library card or student ID card from Humber College. I didn't drive then and I didn't have anything else on me. I furnished him with an address, etc.

He says, *"Wait here,"* and he goes to his car where he presumably calls in a name check to see if I was a trouble maker, drug dealer, known felon or axe murderer. In the back of my mind, I was thinking that a radio check might turn up my name regarding that little incident in High Park a few years back, but thankfully it didn't. I'm being paranoid.

As he's sitting in his car yakking on his radio, Tommy says, *"Didn't you see the patrol car, man? It's friggin' yellow."*

"No I didn't see the friggin' yellow patrol car! I was looking for moving traffic, not some schmuck cop looking for an easy bust."

"Yeah. Well don't thank him for the ticket."

"What'd you mean?"

"When he gives you the ticket, don't say anything like, 'Thank you officer.'"

"Yeah. Like I'm going to thank him for a $22 ticket. Get real."

"I'll bet you'll thank him. I'll bet you five dollars."

"Don't worry. I won't."

"Five bucks says you will."

"Fine. I can use your five bucks to help pay the ticket."

In a moment the officer returns with his ticket all written up for me in surprisingly nice cursive. He start in about obeying the traffic laws and how it's important, especially for cyclists, to come to a complete stop.

In my head I can hear my self saying, "You can either give me the ticket or give me the lecture, but you can't give me both!" The voice in my head was beginning to get louder and louder. I was literally biting my tongue and he droned on and on about the importance of cyclist safety, how many cyclists are killed each year and how we need to heed the signs and other rules of the road.

By this time, I'm straddling my cross bar, with forearms leaning on my handlebars, head hanging lower and lower with each passing minute, just waiting for him to finish. Oh, God, when will he shut up?

Finally, after what seemed like ten minutes, he hands me the ticket and notes that it must be paid within 21 days or I need to plead 'not guilty' and make arrangements for a court appearance, and some other things I don't recall now.

He turns on his heel and as he makes his way back to the cruiser he says, *"You boys have a good night and ride carefully."*

And before I know it, I reply, *"Thank you officer."*

"Five bucks! That's five bucks Horner. I can't believe you thanked him! What a maroon. Oh man. Five bucks, please."

There was no lesson learned here. At that age, there rarely is. I suppose, if pressed, I'd say I learned not to get caught going through a stop sign. But knowing something and doing something, as already pointed out in *The Bottecchia Giro d'Italia,* are rarely the same thing.

———————

"When the spirits are low, when the day appears dark, when work becomes monotonous, when hope hardly seems worth having, just mount a bicycle and go out for a spin down the road, without thought on anything but the ride you are taking.

I have myself ridden the bicycle most during my practice as a physician and during my work in letters. In the morning or the afternoon, before or after work as the mood o'ertakes me, I mount the wheel and am off for a spin of a few miles up or down the road from my country place. I can only speak words of praise for the bicycle, for I believe that its use is commonly beneficial and not at all detrimental to health, except in the matter of beginners who overdo it."

~ Arthur Conan Doyle, on the benefits of cycling
Scientific American, January 18, 1896

The-Bike-To-End-All-Bikes
A Lustful Lad

I love bikes and I love biking almost as much. I've owned mountain bikes, bikes with coaster brakes, a Strumey-Archer drop handlebar Super Cycle Racer from Canadian Tire. I've owned a French Gitane, Tour d'France (purchased at a police auction for $50 and only because I read that's what Jacques Anquetil rode to win the 1964 Tour.) I currently own a Japanese, Univega hybrid. But I haven't mentioned the The-Bike-To-End-All-Bikes. The bike that made me choose it, over a used automobile in college.

I owned my Bottecchia for a couple of years and loved it very much. We'd go on dates to far away places like Terra Cotta, Collingwood or Stratford. We'd spend long weekends together in Montreal or Wiarton. I was in love and I only had eyes for her. But, and here I hang my head in shame, you know how we riders are. I was unfaithful. There, I said it. I was lusting after another. My eyes and (shame of shames) my *hands* wandered! Another had caught my eye.

She was Italian, born in Milan, slim and light – lighter even than my Bottecchia   Giro d'Italia. Olive skin and wide, mountain-road climbing handlebars with a cross stiffener at the stem. She was a Cinelli Supercorsa.

Her hand cut lugs were lovingly brazed onto legendary Columbus steel tubing by skilled Italian craftsmen – maybe even Cino himself, for he actually worked on frames in those days.

The Cinelli hubs were polished to a lustrous gleam. The shifting levers were placed in the ends of the handlebars – the handlebars! Not awkwardly located on the down-tube like 99% of other bikes of the day, such brilliance.

The Campagnolo brakes were lithe but powerful and oh, oh the sloping shoulders of her rakish fork crown … yeah, you know what I'm talking about. You dream about an angle like that. I'm drooling even as I write this.

This was the Samurai sword of racing bikes – nothing extra, nothing wasted. It was sharpened, honed and bereft of every extraneous feature that didn't do a specific job perfectly and elegantly. To press the metaphors further, it was a thoroughbred in the bicycle racing world. It was a specific tool for a specific job, created by masters of their craft.

I first saw her on display at Bloor Cycle. She was sitting by herself, on a little stand that seemed to support her only by her elegant bottom bracket. At first, I thought she looked a little anemic. Maybe a little too thin and wiry. Not strong enough for a real ride by any but the lightest of men or women, but the width of her handlebars and the powerful looking crank set, housed in an over-sized bottom bracket, belayed that notion. This was a bike meant to be ridden hard and long. Not a flaw in the brazed joints. Two tiny lugs brazed to the down-tube solely for the purpose of easing in two Allen screws to secure a water bottle cage. Pure elegance. This was love at first sight. It was even a 58.5cm frame – exactly what I needed.

The price tag – a little piece of cardboard with rounded corners, no larger than a postage stamp, was hanging from the handlebars, just like every other bike in the joint. I looked over my shoulder to see if anyone was watching, then gently blew on it to flip it over. $2,000! This ride was so far out of my snack bracket that I didn't even know a snack bracket of this size existed – remember this was circa 1974. I couldn't afford half that price.

Or so I thought. I rode home and started looking at my limited assets; one blue and white Giro d'Italia, four or five sets of alpine skis (I love skiing almost as much as I love biking), three sets of ski boots, one wooden kayak, one Glen-L "Saboteer" sailboat - as you can see, I loved messing around in boats as well.

If I sold everything I had and added it to the amount I had in the bank I just might have enough.

Now I had to start rationalizing. Even my lustful brain had a modicum of sense. This was a $2,000 machine that I had no real reason to own. My Bottecchia was already more bike than I needed. If I didn't buy the Cinelli, I could buy a used car – and I would have liked a car. I was going to Humber College in those days and was taking the express bus from Islington subway station. It was over an hour and a half commute. But this was a Cinelli Supercorsa!

I started telling myself that this was The-Bike-To-End-All-Bikes. After this bike I'd never need another bike so long as I lived. After all, it really was good for the environment – no costly and polluting fossil fuels need be burned. No carbon dioxide emitted to warm the atmosphere. It was good for my health – all that exercise. For sure I'd be good for my ego – no more be said on that topic. I consoled myself that I didn't drink, take drugs, spend money gambling or on, well, anything really. Further, with this bike, I'd be able to train for hours more each week for skiing! Finally, I didn't have a girlfriend upon whom I could lavish my attentions. So, really, not having this bike began to make less and less sense as the days passed.

Yard Sale

My parents and younger sister went up to the cottage in August. My older sister worked full time and was known to enjoy her week-ends either at the cottage or with friends at Musselman Lake. The time was nigh.

I dragged out all my ski equipment, boats, paddles, PFDs, old comic books, a reel-to-reel tape recorder, a cassette recorder and anything else I had, but no longer "needed," and had my yard sale on the first Saturday of August.

Turns out there had never been a yard sale in my High Park neighbourhood before – or so it seemed. I put up signs on posts and mail boxes. I dropped hand written invitations into the mail slots of most of the neighbours homes – skipping Mrs. Bridget, Widow Kennedy and a couple others. I had a pocket full of coins and small bills for making change. All was ready.

First to arrived were the cops. What's with me and cops?

"Is this all yours?" the officer asks.

"Yep," I replied, "All my stuff."

The cop asks, "Anything stolen?"

"What? No, of course not. It's all mine," I reply.

He walks over to my skis and starts writing down serial numbers and descriptions of the gear. I walk over and ask what he's doing. This gets me an animated lecture from the cop, who for some reason thinks it's necessary to call over his partner, who seemed content to sip Country Style coffee in the passenger seat of the cruiser. Now I'm getting a lecture from these two know-it-alls.

This only attracted the attention of the nosier neighbours who skulked out of their houses and stood on the porches to watch what was going down with the long-haired, hippy-kid the Horner's raised. I could just hear the phone calls from house to house, "The police are at the Horner's. The lad must be in trouble. He's always getting in trouble."

To paraphrase Chandler Bing from Friends, "Could that *be* any less true?" The police had never been to our house for anything I ever did. I'm not saying I didn't do plenty, but I had to imagine the cops had other things to do than follow up on an idiot kid trying to ride a CCM Mustang through the duck pond in High Park or crashing over a boxwood hedge in Hillside Gardens.

The cops and their yellow cruiser, finally left, paving the way for neighbours both nosy and curious to come over and find out what was going on.

I told each as they arrived, that I was having a yard sale – something I'd seen in Michigan on my last trip to see my Uncle Ed and his wife a few months back. Well, the neighbours kind of took to the idea and started looking over my stuff and asking about prices. Cars stopped and passengers and drivers got out to see why everyone was crowded around the house.

By the end of the day, I had disposed of my *"Saboteer"* sail boat (loaded onto the top of a brown, land-yacht sized, Buick Estate Wagon), two pair of skis, one pair of boots, the kayak (which I built in the basement and had to drag out through a window, as It wouldn't come up the stairs, despite all my measuring), the Phillips reel-to-reel recorder, a bunch of Eagles and Valdi 8-tracks, and a couple of shopping bags worth of comic books (I had to, "throw in" a microscope before a neighbours kid would buy the comics). All in all, not bad really almost $600 in my pocket and all that crap out of the way! I still had the Bottecchia and not enough money. The Giro d'Italia had to go.

I put an ad in the Telegram – For Sale, one Italian made racing bike .... Beautifully maintained, etc. ... $400. The ad cost about $6 as I recall and ran for three days. On the final day a phone call came and the bike went for $350. It cost me $600 two years earlier and I felt this was a good price for both parties. Some guy from Hamilton wanted a quality machine for his lad, who was about my age. I gave him a water bottle, some extra rolls of handlebar tape, a couple of spare tires and repair kit, and a handful of specialized tools that would only fit the Bottecchia. I think I even gave him an extra chain. He pulls a wad of cash out of his pocket. It was as round as a *64 pack* grapefruit and secured with a purple elastic band that looks like it came off an asparagus bunch. He peels off seventeen twenties and a ten.

Long story short, I now had enough money and raced down to Bloor Cycle on Monday. The Cino was still there! I tracked down Andrew and gave him my cheque. Such a gracious man. Anyone else would have said that they would have to keep the bike until the cheque cleared, but not Andrew. He wrote up the receipt, walked over to the Cinelli display stand and pulled her down.

He and I went through every feature of the machine. I didn't know about the Cinelli Bivalent hubs which allowed the front and back wheels to be interchanged. I can't exactly remember how, but the rear gear cluster stayed on the frame and you pulled out the hub skew to remove the wheel. For race mechanics, accompanying competitive racers, this meant that they only had to carry one type of wheel arrangement as it would fit the front or back. It also meant they never even had to touch the gears or chain, as they stayed on the frame, completely undisturbed. The whole arrangement was quite clever really.

I also learned that about $200 worth of this machine was the Pino Maroni titanium bottom bracket set, which utilized sealed bearings and even came with its own installation and adjustment tool. (I often wondered about that American made bottom bracket, as I never saw it on any other Cinelli. I suspected, months later, that the bike was a custom order that never got picked up.)

Another thing that always kind of bothered me about the Cino was that the paint job seemed to be only that – a job. Not a multi-layered coating over a flawless primer applied by a skilled artisan. It was more of a coat of paint applied at the end to make one frame look different from another, in the case of my Cino, it was a dull gold colour. Not the best work when compared to many other bikes of the day like Colonago, Massi, Bianci or Pinarello. I even remember the paint on the cross bar, slowly wearing away as the cloth of my pants brushed against it, hour after hour, day after day. No big deal really, for all machines bear the scars of their experience, but no other bike I owned ever did that.

The Cino became my daily ride for about three years. I used it back and forth to work or school on weekdays and Saturday morning century rides with a couple of clubs.

Humility

My word, those club riders go fast - I finally had to drop down to the junior riders where I still struggled to keep up - these guys were FIT! I think back to one of the earlier rides with the "older guys." I was struggling up a steep hill, heading south out of Bolton, about mile 60, on a humid summer's day with the mercury touching 35°C. I was standing on my cranks, wavering up the hill in a 47" gear (42/24) only to be passed like I was standing still, by some sun-tanned, old guy - in the saddle - with a lit cigarette hanging off his bottom lip, a wool jersey with something, "Milano" written across the back and a sweat-stained Colonago cycling cap. I was humbled. I still feel the sting.

Calgary

When I moved to Calgary, the Cino went with me, but like all things, tastes and times change. While there, I sold the Cino to an Italian immigrant who knew bikes, but had not seen a Cinelli since he left Italy for Calgary some years earlier.

I got $800 after adding in a few extras, like tires, the original seat (which I didn't like much and had replaced with a Brooks saddle), a new high-pressure pump, some specialized tools and my old Campy shoulder bag – that old sweat-stained canvas bag seemed to clinch the deal for some reason. I don't know what happened to the new owner or the bike after our transaction. I think I may have caught a glimpse of them once or twice around the reservoir, but I wasn't sure. Lets hope he had many joyful miles and years with that bike. I know I did.

I still had the old Gitane, of course, (the one I picked up for $50 at a police auction) and it was a great bike, but not in the same way the Cino was. The sum of it's parts equaled exactly the sum of it's parts.

When I got back to Toronto, five years later, the first thing I did was run down to Duke's Cycle and have a chat with Gary, who ended up selling me a Miyata mountain bike –

which, while very nice and well made, lacked the soul of the Cinelli. In fact, no other bike I've owned had the soul and/or character of that bike. Unlike the Gitane, the sum of it's parts added up to more than just a bicycle. I'm almost a little teary-eyed thinking about that bike – I really miss her.

Rice Paddy of the Shrine
How to Lose a Bike

If you live in Toronto and you lock your bike *anywhere* but in your living room or handcuffed to your wrist, the odds are good that, one day, you're going to get your bike lifted. It's almost inevitable. You make your best effort with locks and chains, but they were made to be busted, keys and locks just can't be trusted. Even the venerable "U" locks have been cracked. What's a boy to do?

I had just returned to Toronto, after having lived in Calgary for five years and I needed a new bike. I had grown from a trouble-making teen into a relatively stable young man by this time. I went to see my friend Gary Duke at Duke's Cycle and Sports.

Mountain bikes were all the rage, at that time, and Gary had a nice selection of machines. In the end, we landed on a Miyata, a nice Japanese machine with middle of the road pricing, about $600. I was told that Miyata means *Rice Paddy of the Shrine,* in Japanese. I don't know if that's true, but I do know that it's a popular last name in some regions of Japan and the Ryukyu Islands.

This machine was equipped with an upper end Suntour *gruppo di componenti*, and nice gnarly all terrain tires. It used high tensile steel tubing, beautifully brazed lugs and over-sized fork tubes. All black with white letter-ing. To be sure it was heavy, weighing in at 32 pounds, compared to the *Supercorsa* which tipped the scales at a shade over 20 pounds. All in all, though it was a very nice machine, tough and durable.

It became my daily ride for a couple of years, until it disappeared one fine afternoon in Sep-tember.

I was at Ryerson, looking into some part time courses and I had locked the Miyata to a "No Parking" sign. In this case, it was a sign sit-ting at the top of an eight foot steel pole, stuck in the sidewalk. I used one of the early Kryp-tonite U locks which was sold with some sort of guarantee against theft, not that it would have helped much as the thieves didn't break the lock.

As it turns out, the steel post was inserted into a steel collar, itself imbedded in the sidewalk. The collar was immovable, but the sign post could be pulled out of the collar. The thieves just rolled up, lifted out the sign post, slid out my bike and replaced the post.

When I came out of the building, and onto the street, my bike just wasn't there. It was quite a stomach punch. At first I felt violated, then I felt disappointment. That was soon followed with despair and then anger and finally betrayal. I asked around if anyone had seen anything. Nope. No one had seen a thing. How could no one have seen anything!? It was the middle of the day!

I made my down to 52 Division at Dundas and McCaul to report both the theft of my bike and the sketchy sign post. The officer at the desk seemed, uninterested, to say the least. Without even making eye contact he hands over a form, "Fill this out," he says with a few taps of his finger. I feel my pockets for a pen. He seems to notice this and tosses out a Bic extra fine – the one with the polished brass tip, not like the gold coloured plastic ones they sell you today.

I dutifully and sadly sit down on one of the hard plastic chairs and, like Will Smith in Men in Black, struggle to fill out the form on my lap. It becomes quickly apparent, that without the serial number, nothing is going to happen. I had the serial number recorded at home, I just didn't carry it around with me. I fold up the form, tuck it into my shirt pocket, to the Bic back onto the counter and depart. I take the subway home to Castleview manor, bike helmet trailing along behind me like a lost cat following me home.

I related the tale to my neighbour Mike and he tells me about a couple of his bikes that were stolen. I ask him if the cops did anything. "Maybe, but I didn't get either of the bikes back and I never heard from the cops."

He goes on to say that bike theft is almost the perfect crime to commit, if you're so inclined. The cops don't treat the crime as serious, and view bicycles as toys. The bicycle itself isn't the end game for the thief. The bikes are often taken by drug users who only want to sell the bike for their next fix. Any professional bike theft ring would have the stolen bikes shipped quickly to another province in the back of a cube van or quickly dismantled for the value of their components - which aren't stamped with serial numbers and are therefore unidentifiable.

Then, even if a thief gets caught, good luck getting a judge who has any interest in a conviction for some drug addict stealing toys. It just isn't worth them worrying about.

According to a 2014 University of McGill study, only about 2.4% of bikes are recovered of the 2,000 reported stolen in Montreal. - and those are the *reported* cases. The study suggests that some 20,000 bikes are taken every year. The majority of people don't bother to report their bike stolen as they know it isn't worth their time and effort. Astonishingly, something like 7.5% of the people who have their bikes stolen, are despondent and simply give up riding completely.

I wasn't about to give up riding, since I still had my Gitane, but getting my Miyata taken was a real punch in the gut.

Then one day, about the middle of November, I was riding home from work when I saw my Miyata. I was crossing St. Clair, going south-bound down Spadina Rd. The unidentified suspect was sitting at the red light east bound. I pulled to a stop, crossed Spadina and headed back to St. Clair just as the suspect started out across the intersection. I got a good look at the bike. Sure *looked* like my bike.

Now it's not like I had owned the only black Miyata in the City. Gary had mention that he had sold at least a dozen of them just at his store alone. There could be scores of them out there. Still, I decided to follow this guy and see where he went.

What if it was my bike? Should I tackle the guy and make a citizens arrest? I wonder if I should get some cable ties so I could 'cuff him? No. I'd have to stop for that or go home first, then I'd loose him. Should I just find out where he lives and then get Mike to help me steal my bike back, maybe steal it out of his yard, or wherever he kept it. Maybe he keeps it in a locked garage. That's break and enter … a whole other consideration. Should I just confront the guy and tell him I want my bike back?

Whoa. Wait a minute, I'm putting the cart before the horse here. Just follow the guy and see where that takes me.

He continued along St. Clair, past Poplar Plains, past Avenue Road, past the Granite Condo. When he gets to Yonge, he turns south. He continued a couple blocks then turned east, onto Rosehill Ave. He went behind a large apartment building on the north side and locked his bike to a communal rack. In a moment he disappeared inside.

I had to work fast. He might not be going up too many floors. He may live on the north side of the building and might look down and see me looking at his bike.

I laid my Gitane down behind some bushes and nonchalantly strolled to the Miyata. Yep. It sure looked like mine, but it could have been one that just looked like it. I needed to get the serial number from the bottom bracket to be sure. I pulled a pencil and notebook out of my shoulder bag, lugged the Miyata up and over on its side and panic. The serial number isn't on the bottom bracket! What the hell?

I quickly look on the bottom of the seat tube, the back of the head set. Not there. I finally find it on the left side of the seat tube, near the top, where the top tube is brazed to the seat tube. I carefully wrote out the number - NVG00128A6B. I replaced the Miyata as I found it and ran back to the Gitane, laying on its side, behind the bushes. I could almost hear the theme music from Mission Impossible or Man From U.N.C.L.E.

I ride home and drag my bike inside. Wheres that receipt!? Found it! Not too hard really, as I was writing in those days and had a couple of books published by Lone Pine Publishing, so I kept receipts for *everything* that could have *anything* to do with writing bicycle books.

I pulled the notepad out of my shoulder bag and compared the numbers. If they matched, I had my man. I'd call the local police at 53 Division and let them know where they could pick up the perp. Steady now. Careful NVG00149A6B. Bah! It wasn't a match. I was so sure.

So I didn't get my bike that day, or any other day for that matter. It was probably in Saskatchewan by now or dismantled into its component parts and sold piece by piece. I didn't crack the bicycle theft ring, but what a thrill it was to feel the adrenaline start flowing and my blood race as I followed the suspect along St. Clair and onto Yonge Street.

We get too attached to things. We act like everything is going to work out for the best all the time, despite the evidence to the contrary. We see almost everything fall to dust, but we think that everything is so permanent. Everything is only here for a while, then it's gone. We don't "own" anything. We only have it until we lose it, give it away, break it or it gets taken by someone who wants it more.

———————

It's been 40 years since that last story. I'm still cycling regularly and I still own that Japanese-made Univega. I don't ride like I used to; not as hard, not as far and with not as much adventure, but for me, getting on a bike, still brings a tremendous amount of joy. Even if only for a short trip to the office, or a weekend ride along the Don Valley Bike path, just a stone's throw from my home in Riverdale.

About the Author

Horner has been hiking, skiing and pad-
dling throughout Ontario and Alberta for
over 50 years. He's an avid photographer,
cyclist and keen outdoor enthusiast. He's
the author of The Complete Family
Camping Guide and founder of Friends of
Dieppe Park. He is a past member of the
Harbourfront Parks and Open Space
Project, in Toronto.

Pain and Suffering
In Buddhism

Edward Horner

Death and Dying
In Buddhism

Edward Horner

Other Books by Edward Horner

Pain and Suffering in Buddhism

In Pain and Suffering, we explore our special relationship with these two afflictions and look deeply into how our ego drives us ever forward towards disappointment and regret. However we don't leave the reader with just an understanding of how we suffer and why we have pain. We take a serious look at how, with diligence and patience, we can apply a specific program to escape or at the very least, lessen our suffering.

ISBN 978-0-9953161-9-5
Paperback, 110 pp.

Death and Dying in Buddhism

No human being, animal, plant nor smallest microbe manages to escape death. It's the ultimate end of everyone now living or that ever will live. There is no "cure" and no avoiding it, but from a Buddhist perspective, suffering over this inevitability is something we can reduce and maybe even sidestep.

In Death and Dying, Horner gives us hope that we can shake off the fear of death and bring a clear mind to the process.

ISBN 978-1-7771539-0-8

Paperback 108pp.

Wisdom
In Buddhism

Edward Horner

Wisdom in Buddhism

What is wisdom? Who is wise? Can wisdom be developed? These are the questions Horner sets out to answer, from a Buddhist perspective. He manages to avoid convoluted, philosophical discussions, focusing instead on secular, everyday concerns with thoughtful examples and practical applications in a workman-like manner to help the reader better understand the nature of wisdom and how it can be developed.

The author sets forth 12 pillars of wisdom that are easily accessed and applied – not only in Buddhism – but life in general.

- Compassion
- Values
- Education
- Impermanence
- Mental Bias
- Theory of Mind

- Perspective
- Humility
- Life Events
- Compassion
- Concentration
- Emotional Stability

Spoiler alert; with proper intent and focused attention wisdom *can* be developed.

ISBN 978-1-7771539-1-5

Paperback, 377pp.